PLANET HUNTING

RACKING UP DATA AND LOOKING FOR LIFE

ANDY LANGLEY

CONTENT CONSULTANT
SARAH RUIZ
Aerospace Engineer

CAPSTONE PRESS
a capstone imprint

Edge Books are published by Capstone Press,
1710 Roe Crest Drive, North Mankato, Minnesota 56003
www.capstonepub.com

Library of Congress Cataloging-in-Publication Data
Names: Langley, Andrew, 1949– author.
Title: Planet hunting : racking up data and looking for life / by Andy Langley.
Description: North Mankato, Minnesota : Capstone Press, [2019] | Series: Edge books.
Future space | Audience: Ages 8–9. | Audience: Grades 4 to 6. Identifiers: LCCN 2019004844|
ISBN 9781543572704 (hardcover) | ISBN 9781543575163 (pbk.) | ISBN 9781543572780 (ebook pdf)
Subjects: LCSH: Extrasolar planets—Detection—Juvenile literature. | Habitable planets—Juvenile
literature. | Life on other planets—Juvenile literature. | Outer space—Exploration—Juvenile
literature. Classification: LCC QB820 .L36 2019 | DDC 523.2/4—dc23 LC record available at
https://lccn.loc.gov/2019004844

Editorial Credits
Michelle Parkin, editor; Laura Mitchell, designer; Jo Miller, media researcher;
Katy LaVigne, production specialist

Photo Credits
NASA, 22, 27, 28; NASA: Desiree Stover, 25; NASA: Goddard/S. Wiessinger, Cover; NASA/JPL-
Caltech, 17; Newscom: World History Archive, 8, ZUMA Press/NASA, 14; Science Source: European
Southern Observatory, 12, Jerry Lodriguss, 5, Jon Lomberg, 11, Lynette Cook, 7, Richard Bizley, 19;
Shutterstock: MacelClemens, 21

Design Elements
Capstone; Shutterstock: Audrius Birbilas

Printed in the United States   5702

TABLE OF CONTENTS

CHAPTER ONE

BILLIONS OF SUNS

Look up at the night sky. How many planets do you think are out there? You can see five planets without a telescope—Mercury, Venus, Mars, Jupiter, and Saturn. Including Earth, there are eight planets in our **solar system**. They are all **orbiting** around the sun.

Because Earth orbits around it, our sun gets a lot of attention. But there are billions of suns in the universe. A sun is any star that has its own solar system of planets orbiting it. Many of the stars we see in the sky can also be suns. Scientists think there are trillions of planets in space. We call the planets outside our solar system **exoplanets**. Scientists are just beginning to learn about them.

Saturn

Mars

Venus

Mercury

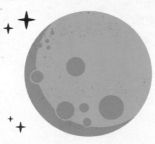

exoplanet—a planet outside of our solar system

orbit—to travel around a sun or a planet

solar system—the sun and all the planets, moons, comets, and smaller bodies orbiting it

SPACE FACT:

There are between 100 and 400 billion stars in our galaxy.

For centuries, **astronomers** have believed that exoplanets existed. But they couldn't prove it. Telescopes were not strong enough to see that far into space.

Then a great breakthrough came in 1995. For the first time, a planet was discovered orbiting a sunlike star. Scientists Michel Mayor and Didier Queloz found this exoplanet by using images and information from the Haute-Provence Observatory in southeast France. The new planet was named 51 Pegasi b. Later the name was changed to Dimidium.

Since then scientists have tracked down nearly 4,000 exoplanets. But this is just the beginning. There are many more exoplanets to find. Scientists are building new and more complex telescopes. Some will be on Earth, while others will be launched into space.

astronomer—a scientist who studies stars, planets, and other objects in space

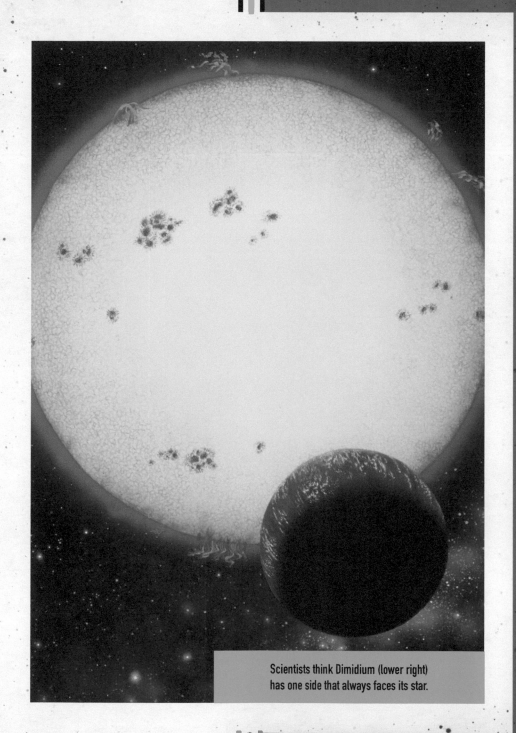

Scientists think Dimidium (lower right) has one side that always faces its star.

Hunting for planets takes a lot of money. The Kepler Space Telescope cost more than $600 million. The Wide Field Infrared Survey Telescope (WFIRST) will cost at least $3.2 billion. WFIRST is set to launch into space in the mid-2020s.

Scientists believe there could be billions of planets that are similar to Earth.

The Next Earth

What does an exoplanet need to have to be considered an Earth-like planet?

Location, location, location. The planet has to be in the right place. It can't be too close to its sun, because it will be too hot for life to exist. If it's too far away, the planet will be too cold.

Just right. The planet has to be about the same size as Earth. It also needs an Earth-sized atmosphere to protect it from harmful radiation.

Water, water everywhere. The planet needs to have a source of water for life to survive.

But the cost is well worth it. If scientists look in the right place, they could find another planet like Earth. But finding a planet like ours won't be easy. It has to have enough water and breathable air to support life. Scientists haven't found a planet like that yet.

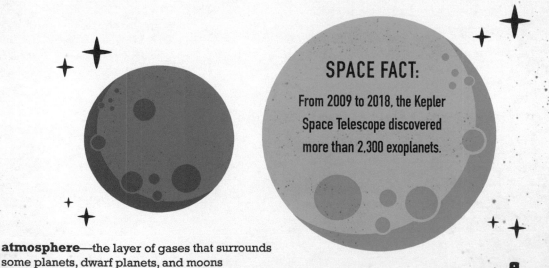

SPACE FACT:

From 2009 to 2018, the Kepler Space Telescope discovered more than 2,300 exoplanets.

atmosphere—the layer of gases that surrounds some planets, dwarf planets, and moons

CHAPTER TWO

HOW TO FIND A PLANET

THE TRANSIT METHOD

Scientists find most exoplanets with the transit method. In this method, scientists use telescopes to closely watch groups of stars. The telescopes identify any exoplanets that cross, or transit, between Earth and a star.

Planets are tiny compared to stars. Even powerful telescopes can't actually see them. The planet blocks some of a star's light as it crosses. The star looks dimmer. The longer the transit lasts, the farther away the exoplanet is.

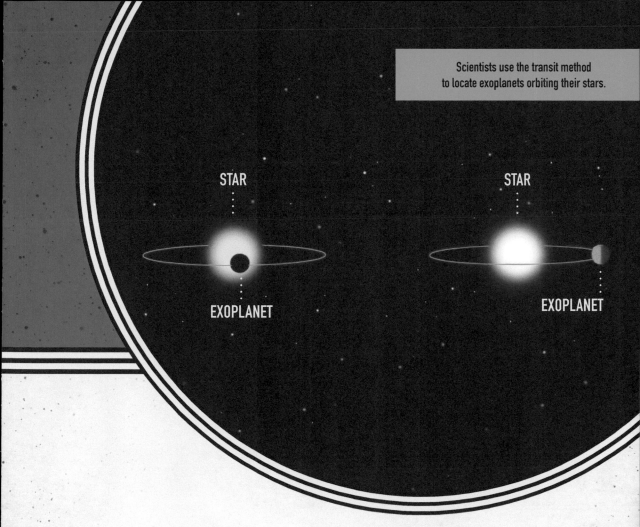

STAR

STAR

EXOPLANET

EXOPLANET

Scientists have discovered more than 3,000 exoplanets using the transit method. But the method does have its disadvantages. For example, a distant planet has to pass directly between the star and Earth for this method to be successful. Some exoplanets will never do this. That is why scientists use other methods to find exoplanets too.

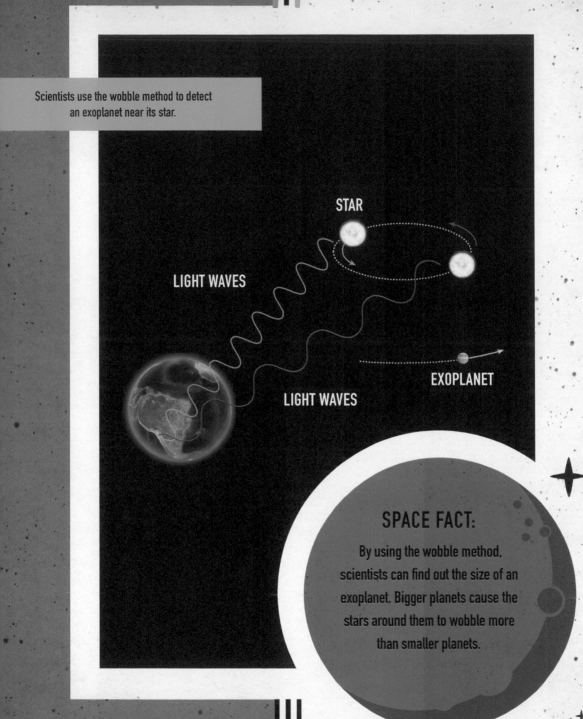

STAR

LIGHT WAVES

LIGHT WAVES

EXOPLANET

SPACE FACT:

By using the wobble method, scientists can find out the size of an exoplanet. Bigger planets cause the stars around them to wobble more than smaller planets.

THE WOBBLE METHOD

Scientists find some exoplanets using the wobble method. The pull of **gravity** keeps planets in orbit around their sun. Planets have a gravitational pull too. This pull appears to slightly move, or wobble, the planet's sun.

Scientists use powerful **spectrographs** to pick up these tiny wobbles. As the exoplanet orbits its sun, the spectrograph monitors the sun's light waves. These waves are squeezed together when the sun moves closer to us. When it moves farther away, the waves stretch out. This makes the sun seem to wobble.

gravity—a force that pulls objects together; the sun's gravity holds Earth and the other planets in orbit around it

spectrograph—an instrument used to record light in space

STAR GLARE

Using powerful telescopes, scientists can see
stars that are billions of miles away. Stars send out
bright rays that telescopes can detect. But exoplanets
are different. They are small, dark, and produce
very little light of their own. Scientists can see an
exoplanet only when light from a nearby star reflects
off the planet's surface.

NASA's Kepler Space Telescope observed sunlike stars and planets during its mission.

But this can cause another problem. Stars create large amounts of light. The glare from this light can make it impossible to detect a tiny planet in the darkness.

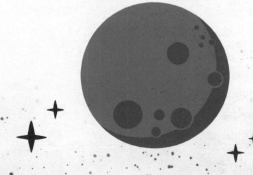

DIRECT IMAGING

How do scientists avoid a star's bright glare when searching for exoplanets? One way is direct imaging. This method allows astronomers to pick up the dim light coming from the exoplanet itself. Scientists use a coronagraph in this method. This small mask is placed inside the telescope. The mask blocks out most of the starlight that comes in. The exoplanet is then visible.

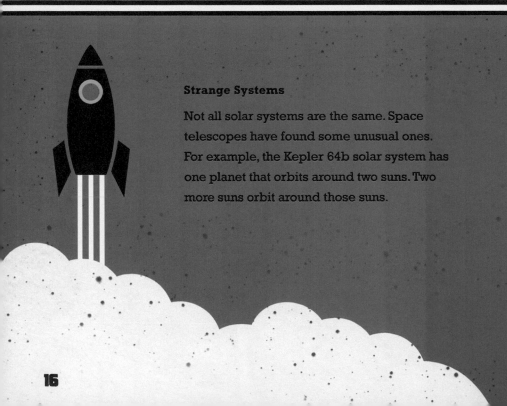

Strange Systems

Not all solar systems are the same. Space telescopes have found some unusual ones. For example, the Kepler 64b solar system has one planet that orbits around two suns. Two more suns orbit around those suns.

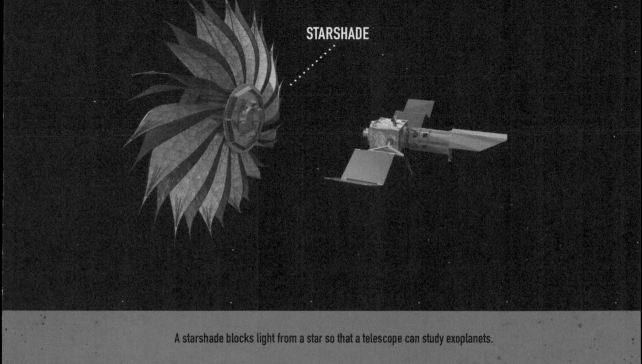

STARSHADE

A starshade blocks light from a star so that a telescope can study exoplanets.

Starshades can also be used. NASA's flower-shaped starshade unfolds like a giant umbrella in space. The starshade is placed between the telescope and a star's bright light. This lets the telescope take pictures of the actual exoplanet.

SPACE FACT:

NASA stands for the National Aeronautics and Space Administration.

CHAPTER THREE

ROCKS, ROGUES, AND HOT JUPITERS

Exoplanets come in all shapes and sizes. Some of them are rocky planets. Some are up to four times bigger than Earth, while others are much smaller. Gas dwarfs are two to four times as big as Earth. These planets have rocky centers surrounded by gas.

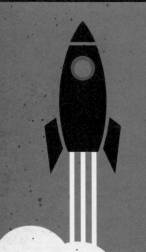

Exocomets and Exomoons

Distant solar systems are full of amazing things besides exoplanets. Some have exocomets. These balls of ice and rock have long tails of dust and gas. Some solar systems have exomoons, which orbit planets. Scientists discovered the first exomoon in 2018.

A planet that does not orbit a star is called a rogue planet.

The biggest exoplanets are called gas giants. One type of gas giant is called a Hot Jupiter. This kind of exoplanet is similar to Jupiter and Saturn, but it's much hotter. Hot Jupiters stick close to their suns—10 times closer than Earth is to our sun. It takes only 10 days for these planets to orbit their sun.

Most planets orbit around a sun. But a few don't orbit around anything. Instead, these planets float around the **galaxy** with no star to heat or light them. These are called rogue planets or orphan planets. Scientists can only spot rogue planets when they pass a star. The star lights up the planet for a few moments.

galaxy—a large group of stars, planets, gas, and dust

WATCHERS IN SPACE

Exciting discoveries are coming from telescopes way out in space. For almost 30 years, scientists have been launching telescopes into orbit. These telescopes have gone far into the universe and found thousands of exoplanets.

One of the most well-known space telescopes is the Hubble Space Telescope. NASA launched the Hubble in 1990. And it's still up there. During its long mission, the Hubble has sent back large amounts of information. It includes many images of exoplanets as well as data about their atmospheres.

A new planet hunter launched into space in 2013. The European Gaia telescope has a big mission. Scientists will use it to survey more than 1 billion stars. Gaia's data will help scientists create the most accurate map of our galaxy. This map will show new planets, comets, and quasars. Quasars are bright objects in deep space. They give off more energy than 100 galaxies put together.

Hubble Space Telescope

TESS

NASA's Transiting Exoplanet Survey Satellite (TESS) joined the planet hunt in April 2018. TESS's journey around Earth takes it close to the moon. The spacecraft's mission is to watch 200,000 of the brightest stars near Earth.

TESS has four wide-angle cameras that detect tiny changes in a star's brightness. This shows that a planet is moving in front of the star. The cameras take exact measurements of these light changes every two minutes.

Scientists have divided up the sky into 26 sections. TESS's cameras will look at one section for 27 days. Then the spacecraft will rotate to the next section. It will take TESS two years to look at all 26 sections in space.

SPACE FACT:

TESS is the first planet-hunting telescope to survey the entire sky. That's an area 400 times larger than the Kepler Space Telescope covered.

CHAPTER FOUR

WHAT'S NEXT?

New space telescopes are becoming more advanced. The Hubble and Kepler telescopes were state-of-the-art when they were launched. The next cutting-edge telescope in space will be NASA's James Webb Space Telescope. The James Webb will be the largest space telescope ever built. When completed, it will be as tall as a three-story house.

SPACE FACT:

Scientists hope that data collected from the James Webb will show what an exoplanet's atmosphere is made of and if humans could survive there.

The gold mirrors of the James Webb Telescope are made to capture infrared light from other galaxies.

The James Webb is scheduled to launch in 2021. Once it is orbiting around the sun, the telescope will unfold a huge mirror. The mirror will catch light from distant parts of space and reflect it inside the telescope. A giant sunshield will protect the instruments inside from the sun's heat. The James Webb will send back images of unknown stars. Scientists hope to also find exoplanets.

In the mid-2020s, NASA plans to launch the WFIRST. The wide field of the telescope's lens and mirror will capture the biggest pictures we have ever seen. While in space, WFIRST's major task will be to hunt for exoplanets. Its wide view will let it watch 100 million stars. Scientists hope WFIRST will find 2,500 new planets.

WFIRST will also measure the **matter** in the universe. Large objects such as galaxies bend the light that passes near the matter. This gives a magnified view of more distant galaxies behind them.

matter—all of the particles that make up the universe

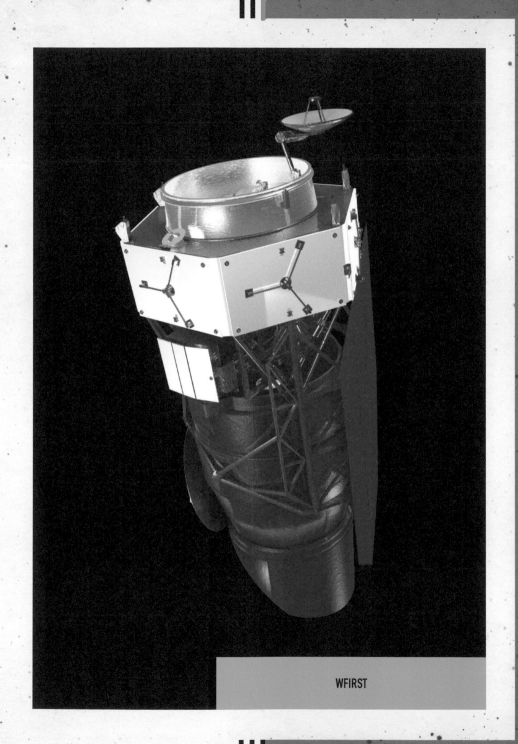

WFIRST

Scientists hope ATLAST will take the clearest pictures yet of what lies beyond the solar system.

THE HUNT CONTINUES

The Hubble Space Telescope will be 40 years old in 2030. By then a new telescope could be doing the Hubble's job. The proposed Advanced Technology Large Aperture Space Telescope (ATLAST) could take pictures up to 2,000 times clearer than Hubble.

ATLAST will be the most powerful space telescope ever built. It will look deeper into space than previous missions. It will also examine the atmospheres and surfaces of exoplanets, looking for water, oxygen, and other signs of life.

So far we haven't found another planet like Earth. But scientists are planning missions to gather more information about these other worlds. The hunt for exoplanets goes on.

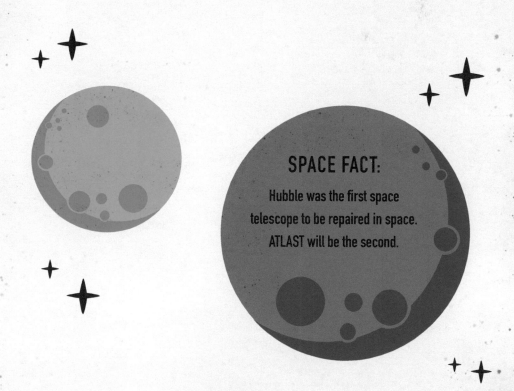

SPACE FACT:

Hubble was the first space telescope to be repaired in space. ATLAST will be the second.

GLOSSARY

astronomer (uh-STRAH-nuh-muhr)—a scientist who studies stars, planets, and other objects in space

atmosphere (AT-muh-sfeer)—the layer of gases that surrounds some planets, dwarf planets, and moons

exoplanet (EK-soh-plan-it)—a planet outside of our solar system

galaxy (GAL-uhk-see)—a large group of stars, planets, gas, and dust

gravity (GRAV-uh-tee)—a force that pulls objects together; the sun's gravity holds Earth and the other planets in orbit around it

matter (MAT-ur)—all of the particles that make up the universe

orbit (OR-bit)—to travel around a sun or a planet

solar system (SOH-lurh SISS-tuhm)—the sun and all the planets, moons, comets, and smaller bodies orbiting it

spectrograph (SPEK-troh-GRAF)—an instrument used to record light in space

READ MORE

Kruesi, Liz. *Finding Earthlike Planets. Space Exploration.* New York: AV2 by Weigl, 2019.

Orr, Tamra B. *Space Discoveries. Marvelous Discoveries.* North Mankato, MN: Capstone Press, 2019.

Simon, Seymour. *Exoplanets.* New York: HarperCollins Publishers, 2018.

INTERNET SITES

Facts about exoplanets
https://www.ouruniverseforkids.com/exoplanets/

What Is an Exoplanet?
https://spaceplace.nasa.gov/all-about-exoplanets/en/

INDEX